From Stepney to London
I (we) seek God's blessings

Ilena Newby

Grosvenor House
Publishing Limited

All rights reserved
Copyright © Ilena Newby, 2022

The right of Ilena Newby to be identified as the author of this
work has been asserted in accordance with Section 78
of the Copyright, Designs and Patents Act 1988

The book cover is copyright to Ilena Newby

This book is published by
Grosvenor House Publishing Ltd
Link House
140 The Broadway, Tolworth, Surrey, KT6 7HT.
www.grosvenorhousepublishing.co.uk

This book is sold subject to the conditions that it shall not, by way of
trade or otherwise, be lent, resold, hired out or otherwise circulated
without the author's or publisher's prior consent in any form of binding or
cover other than that in which it is published and
without a similar condition including this condition being imposed
on the subsequent purchaser.

A CIP record for this book
is available from the British Library

ISBN 978-1-80381-290-8

DEDICATION AND ACKNOWLEDGEMENTS

Dedicated to Muma and Pa, Leah (aka Aneita Downie), Aunty Lou, Aunty Teacha, and cousins in the district.

Cousin Edna Downie (Graham), cousin from Stepney District, a true mentor in my life.

Cousin Josephine was like an aunt, a mother figure, someone who was always there with a listening ear. Who could ask for more? May she rest in eternal peace.

To Pamela Wesley (a secondary school friend) and Leaford Stewart (aka 'Shorty'/'Shortie'). Pamela and Shorty both helped sort out accommodation for my son and me.

Friends along the way:

Sister Joseph (original Ital Queen)

VF (secondary school mate until now)

SR (original Ital Queen)

KRC (Lavender Hill Secondary School)

MLK (secondary school)

SL (secondary school)

HM (secondary school)

CC (may this Queen RIP)

J and D (work colleagues I've known since 1980, who I was with at the DHSS)

Dixon, an original friend of the family, someone who was always there, painter, driver (what you would call a handy friend and family)

More Lavender Hill School possies, some now retired and living abroad (JW, CN, JH, FT, SS and MB)

Sir Coxone (who once lived in Goulden House), an encourager to move forward, advice some of us welcomed. He was one of the original sound system operators in England.

Sis Winifred Rhule (Ocho Rios, Jamaica) was a big sister and mother figure (RIP)

Nuff respect for all my favourite nieces and nephews (they know who they are)

To my three children, and my grandchildren,

Apologies to my children, who I believe I may not have been the best mother to as a one-parent family. I apologise for those who entered into our lives to disrespect and take liberties. God, not sleeping I did my best, but it was not an easy road. I wish there were schools on how to raise children. I can really say, though, that the Almighty was always there. It was God's footprints in the sand carrying us.

Word-power-wisdom – Peter Tosh; listen to his words in all his songs.

CONTENTS

Dedication and Acknowledgements v

Chapter One: Early Childhood 1

Chapter Two: Belville Primary School 13

Chapter Three: Lavender Hill School 17

Chapter Four: Goulden House 28

Baby Mothers for Convenience 38

Chapter Five: Me, Myself and I 39

Chapter Six: Coming to America 41

Chapter Seven: Back Home 44

Chapter Eight: My Children and Grandchildren 55

Keep That Someone 59

CHAPTER ONE

EARLY CHILDHOOD

My childhood memories of growing up in Stepney are full of excitement. One could say I was a little tomboy running around with my older brothers and cousins. My older cousins used to sit on the wall overlooking Auntie Gatty Berry's home up in Berry Hill, waiting for her to call us for food. She lived by herself. Her cooking was out of this world and she was always 'feeding the 5,000'. The partitioning wall adjoined to ours had a custard-apple tree which bore some sweet custard apples. She warned us not to pick them, but me being me, I watched these custard apples, picked one and ate it, as I did not want the birds to beat me to it.

I especially remember Uton (Aston Downie) telling us Anansie stories about Brother Anansie, and Sister Tukuma stories that arrived from West Africa. That is how we entertained ourselves up in the hills listening to the night crickets and watching peenie wallies and rat bats flying around us. We welcomed when it was a full moon, as we did not have to use bottle lamps and torches.

When I visited my other relatives who were nearer the square, Aunty Teacha, I would listen to Louise Bennett advertising cocoa malt and singing folk songs. There were also songs, like 'Pepsi Cola went to town, Coca Cola knock him down, carrying him to Fanta fix him up'. Our skipping game was 'Room for rent, apply within; when I run out, you run in'. Jacks, gigs and marbles games were also some of my entertainments as a child growing up.

Teacher James and his family had proper lights going up to their house and they had a TV. Bottle oil lamps and tin lamps were our flashlights. I can now laugh about an early morning incident when Leah got us up early to walk from up the hill to meet Miss Alice Newby outside Mr Tai's shop to catch the North Liner into Charlton and Brown's Town. Philip was in the front and held the bottle oil lamp, I was in the middle and Rodney ('Chilli') was at the back. As we took a shortcut through Belgium Garden, Philip dropped the bottle oil lamp and ran back up Berry Hill saying he'd seen a *duppy*, leaving Rodney and me running and bawling up the hill. It must have been about 6 am. Leah had to then take us to the Square to meet Miss Alice.

Some of the tricks they would play on us when we had our meals included telling us to look up at the ceiling telling as there was a rat there. When we looked up, then down again, there was no food left on our plates. They'd eaten it all! Some of the food was run down, with yam dumpling and green banana and Sunday rice and peas with cow skin or chicken. When they tricked me out of my food, I was prompted to start cussing at an early age. As far as I can remember, I've not messed with anyone's food.

Cousin Rodulph was the quiet one, who was always curious about where we came from, who our ancestors were and who is buried where and what their names were. Muma would tell us everything, including how they came to live and own land in Berry Hill. They were from a place called Bensonton, on the border between Clarendon and Saint Ann. They settled in Saint Ann when their mother passed away, so their father, Pupa Berry, bought the land in Berry Hill.

My Grandfather Downie's roots can be traced back to Bethany, Saint Ann, and also Portland, where I believe they were farm owners. They also owned Brooman Hill in Stepney. We still have family in Clarendon whom some years ago we met up with in North London. I felt like the ancestors were already living within me. Aunty Gatty Berry is my grandmother's sister; the other sister's name is Aunty Vick (Victoria) who lived up on the hill as you are going into Banzle. Some would call the place 'Bowling Land'.

As a child I used to be very sickly. Sometimes I would say to Muma, 'Look at that girl skipping in the yard with little fowls behind her.' My grandmother would then say she'd lost a daughter in her teens (Aunty Freda). There were more encounters with the unknown (i.e. seeing other things). My grandparents were concerned about me, so they sought spiritual advice. One of the neighbours told my grandparents, aunt and cousins to boil banana in the skin and let me drink the water. Come to think of it, I probably was lacking some sort of iron. I find our older generations to be highly skilled when it comes to being herbalists. Another one of our neighbours I remember to this day is Miss Clemmy and two of her children, Johnny and Joyce. When I went back to Jamaica in 1985, Miss Clemmy reminded me of the time my grandmother called me and I hid and said to Miss Clemmy in Jamaican Patois, '*Nu tel ere sey mi deh ova ya ma.*' I was warned that if I kept on running up and down Berry Hill, I would one day '*bruk out mi toe*'. That's exactly what happened to me. We used to tease the neighbour's dog from Friendly's house. The dog came out, running at us, bit my heel and my toe came out. My grandmother said, '*Si mi waan yu.*'

My grandmother was like a tree of wisdom. She would say things like 'Not every drum that beats, you should dance to', 'Foolish *dawgs* bark after flying birds', 'Yu turn your rump up to *filt* on the righteous and every bit comes back and daub you', 'When your friends are jumping on two feet, try jumping on one, 'Don't envy anyone for what they have, 'cause you don't know how they get what they have', 'Learn to dance at home before you dance abroad' and 'Empty barrels *mek* the most noise'. I can now relate to the poem by Milton Smalling, 'She Looks Like Maroon Nana', in memory of Mr and Mrs Downie. Our grandmother was everything said in the poem.

Muma would always make coffee with a piece of bread or crackers to give to farmers on their way to their ground (field). Our older generations could tell the rising of the sun and where it set. They would tell you when and where it would rain. I believe that this knowledge, instilled in us as children from the Caribbean, was what carried us through when we came to Foreign. As much as they did not want to send us to Foreign, they knew they had to let go.

Grandmother never came down from Berry Hill; I now realise that she suffered from arthritis in her knees. Once you were up the hill, everywhere was flat, so you could move around freely.

I remember going over to Calderwood with all the cousins, my two brothers, my aunt and my grandfather to plant ground; the younger ones would have been chauffeur-driven, sitting in the donkeys' hampers as we cruised past the Calderwood tank and Kenneth Hyde Post Office.

We raised cows, goats, pigs, fowls and rabbits. At a young age we were milking cows and goats. My Auntie Lou was a hard-working lady. She not only worked over at Calderwood, but also on the land up on Berry Hill. I remember we used to cultivate all kind of fruits and vegetables to sell in the markets or on trucks to be shipped abroad. Grandfather Papa would sometimes stop off at Miss Pearl and Mass Verse's shop for a shot of white rum and water. As I sat on the pavement waiting for him, he would let me have a small Red Stripe beer. When we reached the top of Berry Hill, my grandmother would cuss him about giving me Red Stripe beer to drink. I liked it though! You can take me out of the country, but you cannot take the country out of me.

Calderwood, the neighbouring district, was where my other grandparents lived Mass Johnnie Newby with his wife, Miss Alice Newby. They had a son together by the name of Vincent Newby who emigrated to England in the early 1950s with his wife, Lurlin. They had three children: Johnny, Peter and Shirley. Miss Alice's nephew, Teddy Archer, lived with them at Calderwood. That was the house we spent the night in before coming to England.

My other grandmother, Ann Brown, lived with a man called Sammy in a place called Shamfield at the bottom of the street where my brother Rodney ('Chilli') was born. It has been reported that there were only three grandchildren born on Berry Hill: Big Cousin Leah, who belonged to Aunty Lou, my brother Philip (Hylton Lee) and Little Lena, as they would call me. My other cousins, who I remembered also came to London and lived up Brooman Hill next to Aunty Teacha, are Cousins Edna, Ena, Keith (aka 'Dakkie') and Albert. There are loads of other cousins, some names I cannot remember, who were born in Stepney District.

I attended Stepney All Age School, now known as Bob Marley Primary and Junior High School, at the age of five. The reason was that Teacher James told Cousin Leah that if so much cussing (I used to hear it from my older cousins and Aunty Lou, who people used to tease) could come out of a little girl's mouth, then send her into school. From what I can remember I was a bright student, reciting poems such as a 'I Wandered Lonely as a Cloud' by William Wordsworth ('a host of golden daffodils') and The Wind by Robert Louis Stevenson ('I saw you toss the kites on high, And blow the birds about the sky').

My first teacher was Miss Issac, who had two granddaughters, Sandra and Joy Issac. There was an American teacher by the name of Miss Sutherland and Teacher James's wife, Miss Ralph. Their children were Jen, June, Trevor and Tom. School was fun and exciting. Stepney School was always an outstanding school where children attended from neighbouring districts such as Prickly Pole, Rhoden Hall (aka Nine Miles), Calderwood, , Hessle Castle, Sterling and around Balentyne.

If I had I remained in Jamaica I would have gone on to St Hilda's High School in Brown's Town. We were not allowed to be late for school, otherwise Teacher James would stand outside the school gate telling us to stretch out our hands to get a beating before going in. So I would run back home to avoid getting beaten. I would follow Aunty Gatty to her ground round Banzle. I remember bringing in fruits from the trees to give to the teachers so I would be in their good books, which I was.

Stepney Baptist Church was, and still is, famous for all types of entertainments: harvest time, baptism, watch nights, and many more. After Sunday School we would race down the hill into Miss Naomi shop, with our Sunday School offerings, to buy mint balls, Stagga Backs and drops.

One of the first records I ever heard made in Stepney was performed in school by some children, including Cousin Keith Downie. It was about a hog that died in Shiloah and it was Sammy with the grey beard who ate the hog's head. It went to number one, but I don't know what happened to the song thereafter.

Lunches in school were prepared by a neighbour, Miss Emeline. Some of the foods were bulgur rice, cornmeal dumpling, yam and meat kinds. We would also queue up for our calcium drink made with milk powder. We had a few water fountain in the school yard for when we were thirsty. At the back of my class were garden beds where we learnt agriculture. We would mainly plant small things, like Gungo peas, red peas, carrots and other small items, which were part of our lessons. This was one lesson I was good at, as I used to go to the family farms during holiday times. I also had my own little patch where I would plant corn, sweet potatoes, tomatoes, and many more vegetables.

At Easter time you would find me with my brothers and cousins *hissing* kites on Brooman Hill. Months before the next festive season, which was Christmas, the district would be painting houses, stones around flower beds, and tree trunks, and breaking rock stones to gravel the roads. While doing so the older folk would start singing, '*Guh dun a Manwell Road, gal, and bouy fi guh bruk rock stones, bruk dem one by one, bruk dem two by two, mash yu hand nuh cry.*' Then came Christmas. All the way to New Year's Eve there were entertainments.

The Square in Stepney was always bustling, with Miss Cousin Dinah's shop, Miss Naomi's Maxine and Miss Little's, Miss Pearl and Mass Verse's— that was the shop that Bob and his mother used to live and work in—Mr Tai's shop, with his wife Miss Norah and children, Precious and Earl Tai. Their shop is now owned by Menzie, and Cousin Pam Menzie is the son of Aunty Dear, who once lived in Peckham, London.

Over at Calderwood was, and still is, our main post office, now also named Cedella Booker Post Office.

The Downies played an important role in Stepney, especially the men, cousins and aunts. Holiday times were fun, going to Aunty Teacha and her husband and children's farm at Bentaline. Cousin Edna was more on the business side, running the shop at the bottom of Brooman Hill along with her sister Ena. That's where I would get my drops and Bustamante or Stagga Backs. I use to play jacks outside one of my friend's shops. They were the Lawrences, some of whom were Katie, Larry, Elizabeth and Bev. On Mother Miller Hill were residences of Aunt Zen, the Barratts, Taylor Bye and George Miller, and Miss Neita. Miss Neita was a teacher in Stepney School. She was my last teacher before I left Jamaica, and this prompted me to fundraise for the school. Her husband was a sanitary inspector in the district. Miss Olive was one of the district police officers, also Mass Lattie, Miss Vashti's son and Cush's brother. Miss Olive's house was based just before you got to the Williams's house and the parish tank over in Calderwood.

In 1962 Jamaica gained independence from Britain, so I was born a Commonwealth citizen. I remember that day. Everyone who could make it came out to Stepney School to celebrate. We were given a cup containing a pen, sweeties and a small flag, black gold and green. There was dancing in the school, and on the street we sang 'Jamaica Marching On'. It rained slightly and I fell down and cussed the people behind me, saying they'd pushed me down, as we marched over to Calderwood and Sterling. Back in Stepney Square there were banjos, guitars, drums and sound systems, with a maypole and a merry-go-round. The older folk danced Quadrilles, while the younger generation danced Ska and Bluebeat, which are now used throughout the island for hotel entertainments.

After independence we started to see an exodus of families. They seemed to be disappearing from out of the district. Miss Whosee and some of my cousins were no longer around. Windrush here we come!

Only the immediate household knew we were going to *'farin'*, as they would call it. We were not allowed to say anything to anyone when we were leaving. At the end of 1964 two strange-looking people appeared in Stepney and one over in Calderwood: Cousin Josephine, Miss Coolie in Stepney and Miss Lurlin in Calderwood. Josephine came out to sort out Joy, her daughter's, papers, and not knowing, Miss Coolie came to sort out my two brothers' and my papers. It was then we were told that Miss Coolie was our mother. She stayed over in Calderwood at Mass Johnnie and Miss Alice.

Rodulph and Joy then left for England in March 1965. During that time in Berry Hill our relative placed down a glass of water with the white of an egg. It was Easter time and whatever showed up in the glass told them your future, which I found very mystical, as we saw a ship, which signified us travelling. There was also the plant in the garden. When you walked past it or touched it, the leaves would shrivel up. This they called 'shame mi lady'. All these took place on Good Friday.

It was November 1965, and we had to spend our last night over at Calderwood with our other grandparents, Mass Johnnie and Miss Alice Newby. That November evening was going to be the last time I would ever see my Grandmother and Grandfather Downie. As the day broke, my two brothers and I were on our way to Palisadoes Airport in Kingston, Jamaica. The journey was pleasant but there was this sadness that has sat within me for the rest of my life, knowing that I was leaving my grandparents, cousins and aunts and that I would never set eyes on some of them again in this life. They managed to force me onto the BWIA flight bound for London. Tears were streaming everywhere as I wondered how it would be to know my parents for the first time in my life. I can remember my big cousin, Leah, crying as they boarded us onto the plane. We landed for fuel in Nausa, Bahamas, then continued on to the USA. We got off and were escorted into the lounge as we waited for the plane to be serviced.

There were other children who we talked with, some with buns and cheese, some with crackers and biscuits. Yes, we were all going to be joined with our parents or guardians in the United Kingdom. As a matter of fact, when we landed in the USA, I thought I *was* in England, only to be told that we had a long journey to make, at least eight more hours, before we arrived there. As we boarded the flight I was placed at the end seat, Rodney in the middle and Philip ('Lee') at the window. I was crying, and when the air hostess asked what was the matter, I gave out, "*Mi belly a hot mi.*" They gave us sick bags in case we felt sick. We were well taken care of on the flights.

We finally landed safely at London Heathrow Airport. We were escorted to the waiting area by a man who worked for BWIA, who made sure we were handed over to the right parents. A man and woman met us and we were told they were our parents. We got into a taxi, which took us to Shelgate Road, Battersea. The weather was cold, but Miss Cook in Jamaica had made me a winter suit for the cold weather. They unpacked our belongings, as we shared a *grip* (suitcase) between the three of us. We were introduced to our British-born siblings. Before we'd left Jamaica, our grandmother had sent us to a lady named Miss Curry, who had given us a reddish/brown substance that looked like dirt and Bissy tea. We were told that our parents should boil it for us when we landed, but it was never given to us.

My brother Rodney who left Jamaica with me in 1965. May he RIP.

My two brothers and I were the eldest of six children to our mother. They'd sent for us, as our grandparents were getting on in age and there was no one to take care of us. They also had in mind for us to become housemaids in England. My mother soon received a telegram informing us of the passing of Grandmother Downie. The uprooting of us to London had taken its toll on Muma.

Everything was so strange: the coldness, the factory-looking houses and the bleakness. It was a very indescribable experience. We, the Windrush generation were never welcomed into this society.

My mother showed me how to use a gas cooker. She had a washing machine but showed me how to fill the bath and wash out clothes, and they had better be clean otherwise I would have to redo them! I was shown how to clean the stairs, from the top, with a dustpan and broom. Those were some of my chores. My brothers use to singe off chicken hair and then season and cook the chickens. When it was very cold I had to take clothes to the laundry to wash and dry. We were constantly reminded that we were Jamaican-born, and not as privileged as our siblings born in the UK. We were threatened with deportation if we dared comment on the bad treatment toward us. Imagine, we were facing hostilities indoors and throughout society. I sometimes have to smile when I remember the food the British-born ate: things like baked beans, spaghetti, sausages, bacon burgers, fish fingers (proper English). They would give us boiled eggs and bread and fried dumplings. They did not realise that we had the best nourishment in our foods, otherwise they would have made sure we did not get it.

When I came over I was very tiny, so we, the three girls, were the same size in clothes. My mother bought three dresses in the same pattern but different colours. One of my siblings wanted my colour, so I was told to give it to her—Cinderella comes to Battersea, London. After talking to some of my other relatives and friends who had come over to join parents, I got to understand that they received more or less the same treatment. Some of our parents or guardians did not want to accept that we, who came over, should by any means excel above our English siblings. Some would say things like 'How did you manage to get such a job?' They did not have our interests at heart. There was so much division and conflict among the siblings, caused by our parents. Would you believe that as returnees back to the Caribbean they took some of that mentality over to inflict on the native people on the island? Some were even told to vacate where they had been living all their lives. They went back to Jamaica with some kind of unjust attitude from time spent in Foreign. I think some were in shock, as the Jamaica they'd left was not the same one they went back to. You can fool some of the people some of the time, but not all of the time. My mother would send me and my two sisters to Northcote road Baptist church Sunday school and evening service. I can remember meeting up with some of my other cousins who came to England before us, cousin Horace was one of them who lived on St. Johns Hill Drive, Rodulph was based on Harbut Road, Joy was living in Balham on Fernside road, then moved to St. James Drive. I was sent to Joy's mother Josephine Shelly to have my hair done. I then met up with some more of my cousins from Jamaica some came before we came and the rest followed after. They were cousin Edna, Ena, Keith aka (Dakkie), Albert and Frankie. The Downie's Glenda, Freda and their other siblings. Wandsworth common was where we would go and play on the swings and slides. We would also go to Granada cinema on a Saturday to watch Bugs Bunny show. My first seaside trip with Northcote Road Baptist church was at Little Hampton. I remember standing on the shore looking at the sea and thinking how far Jamaica was from where I was standing. I fell asleep on the way back. It was myself and one of my younger siblings that went.

CHAPTER TWO
BELVILLE PRIMARY SCHOOL

Shelgate Road, Battersea

Northcote Road Baptist Church

Shelgate Road, off Northcote Road, is no more than a five-minute walk to Belleville Primary School.

Everything was strange. The school was separated into two buildings: one for girls and the other building for boys.

The headmistress at Belleville School was a very pleasant lady by the name of Miss Cox. I remember my class teacher saying that she was from Israel and she would have to go back to fight for her country. She taught us an Israeli song, which I have completely forgotten.

These are some of the names of others that still stick in my memory: CB, RP, AM, RR, JJ, LM, MW, JS, MH, DH, JR, SR, VD and MD.

I was always chatting Patwa in classes. Hey, everything was completely new, such as drinking milk with a straw from a small bottle. You were offered two biscuits with your milk. We sat in the hall to have our milk and biscuits. We did apparatus, climbing over some wooden horses then falling down on mats. During that short space of time spent in Belleville I managed to win a merit award through making progress.

Certificate of merit from Belleville School

In February 1966 I was sent home from school, as the teacher noticed I was covered with measles, which was a very uncomfortable experience. My mother gave me some medicine to take, but I kept on scratching myself, which then caused sores to break out. After a week or so I was sent back to school.

Back in Belleville Primary we learnt to play the recorder as part of our music lessons. Coming from diverse backgrounds, there were lots of playground activities. Across the road from the school was the home of my secondary school friend VF, where we would meet up to go to Wandsworth Common with our younger siblings.

CHAPTER THREE
LAVENDER HILL SCHOOL

After spending seven months in Belleville Primary School, I went on to Lavender Hill Secondary School in September 1966. The next month I would be twelve years old. My mother walked with me on Northcote Road, then onto Battersea Rise, Eccles Road then to Lavender Hill, opposite the police station, where she saw two sisters going into school and asked them if I could walk with them. She did not take me into school like some other parents. Up until this day I remember the sisters with whom I walked, as they are now active in the church community (Life Tabernacle).

All the new first-years lined up in our uniforms: grey jumpers, grey skirts, blue blouses, black shoes and white socks. As our names were called out, we were then taken to our classes. There were four classes—Q, R, S and T. I was placed in Class S. During break times we would mingle with the other classes. There were also times we would share subjects with those classes, which made us become friends with the other girls. We also made friends with some of the older girls. Until this day some of us still remain friends.

Don't think that it is just now that the weave came about; I and some other girls were sporting weaves. Mine was done by an older cousin who was a qualifying hairdresser.

We would follow some of the older girls, rolling up our skirts above our knees and rolling them back down before we entered our homes.

Me and a friend from Lavender Hill in the grounds of Hampton Court

School activities in Lavender Hill consisted of 75% of us from the Caribbean, including other ethnicities. We played netball and rounders and did running, which took place on the tracks in Battersea Park. There were also Marchants Hill, Surrey, outdoor activities, in which we did cross-country running in the winter, which was so cold that some of us hid in the changing rooms, frightened to go out into the cold weather. The physical education (PE) teachers would come into the changing rooms telling us to get out and take part in the games. Schools from all different boroughs would also attend. There were normally two coach loads from Lavender Hill School.

Sometimes arguments would break out on the coaches. We called it banter. Fighting would take place, then the teachers would threaten us with detention. Some of the rival schools included the famous Mayfield, Garratt Green, Southfields, Marion Thornton, Ensham and Battersea County. The best netball players were MS and CN, and in the year above it was CH, someone you would not mess with unless you wore some kind of body protection. MM, LS and U were outstanding netball players a couple of years above us. It did not make sense to introduce JW to any kind of sports, as she was bound for Hollywood fame and fortune. GR was extremely good at all kinds of sports due to her height, but she was not the flavour of the school, as she seemed to upset or bully almost everyone.

Lavender Hill had a reputation, due to it consisting of so many Windrush generation children. Outsiders would name it the 'School for Unmarried Mothers'. Outside the school gates you would be sure to find others from schools from around the way, like Spencer Park, Tennyson, Shillington, William Blake and some of the boys from Battersea County, which was a mixed school and has now been renamed Harris Academy. During some school plays Miss Shortoe would ask certain boys hanging around to help us with activities. There were lots of plays that took place before holiday times. In one of the plays a group of us girls freshly out of Jamaica went on stage to sing 'Shine Eye Gal', a Jamaican folk song. We did some of the acting, which made the audience roll over with laughter. The girls who took part in this were DS, YC, OB and myself.

At dinner times, even though most of us had school dinners, there was Sid's shop across the road from the school where we would all go to buy his crusty rolls and cheese fillings. No one really took much notice of the cat in the shop.

Once a week we would have swimming at Latchmere Swimming Baths. Up until this day I cannot swim due to an experience in the swimming baths. We were given floats in the shallow end, but I took my fast self, trying to follow some of the other girls who were already swimmers. I tried to go further to the deep end and had to be rescued by the swimming instructor.

Tennyson School, off Queenstown Road, had a section where we did cookery and home economics. It was nice sharing some of the foods with each other. Most of us told jokes from early childhood memories of Jamaica we would share, especially coming from JH from Guy's Hill, St Catherine, and VF from Bog Walk, also St Catherine.

There was no doubt about talent. This song was made up from watching *Bonanza*: 'Here come the stars of *Bonanza*, Horse Ben, Little Joe and Cartright, Big foot horse *bruk im rass* couldn't ride a horse, Ben Cartright caught a fight upon a Friday night, One for the gun and two for the fight *Bonanza*.' Another joke from JH was that a country girl went to Kingston with her mother. She'd never seen electric lights before. When it was getting dark, the light turned on and the country girl said, 'Muma, Muma, *luk moon pon stick*.' The mother replied, 'Yu too dam fool; it's call "elastic" light'. Some areas in Jamaica were more built-up than the hills I came from. Pronunciation of words was a little challenging due to the facts that one word can sound so different. For example, when we were in the playground, we would ask each other, did you watch the 'flim' show instead of saying film. Different dialects. Mind you, even though a lot of us were from the country, we would still style it off by acting Kingstonians: for instance, when asked how much we'd paid for our sweets and rolls, we would say 'sharling' instead of shilling.

Our headmistress, Mrs Broadley, spent some time in Jamaica on the exchange teaching programme. These are some of the Lavender Hill teachers I remember, along with their teaching roles: Miss Wise was our form teacher; Mr Longhan, our art teacher (a student by the name of B. Wall was an outstanding artist and I would not be surprised if she has now become an art teacher); Mr Drasak was the science teacher (I still remember using the Bunson burner); Miss Wright, our drama and English teacher (in the building opposite the car park we would have drama, dancing and poetry classes); Miss Fernando was one of the music teachers; Miss Diddieh taught cookery and home economics; and Mr Mensah, one of our maths teacher. I had a go at the German class; I can remember a few words but I did not get very far with it so I did another subject instead.

School meals were shepherd's pie, steak pies, green peas, carrots, swede, roly poly with jam and custard, and apple turnover. We would sometimes queue up for afters. These meals were always in the middle hall; so was the canteen. I remember just one black canteen staff, compared to now with the changes in catering plus the different nationalities of food.

Miss Stroud was the needlework teacher. Her class was the last I attended before my mother told me to leave and find full-time work. Some of us, including myself, were already planning to leave our homes, so we talked about nursing careers, air hostess jobs, or even joining the army—any career away from home.

Secondary school classmates training as nurses after leaving Lavender Hill

When I left Lavender Hill, I left with seven CSEs (Certificate for Secondary Education). I also had a Certificate for English-Speaking Language (see certificates below) before I left Jamaica. I was so bright that Miss Neita, my last teacher, wanted to put me forward for the spelling bee contest, but some of that was lost when I came over to England due to stress. But still I rise.

ENGLISH SPEAKING BOARD

President: SIR MICHAEL REDGRAVE

This is to CERTIFY that

ILENA NEWBY

was awarded the

SENIOR GRADE INTRODUCTORY CERTIFICATE

at GOOD PASS level

OF THE BOARD'S EXAMINATIONS IN SPOKEN ENGLISH

Christabel Burniston

DIRECTOR OF EXAMINATIONS.

DATE 29th March, 1971

ENGLISH SPEAKING BOARD

President: SIR MICHAEL REDGRAVE

This is to CERTIFY that

ILENA NEWBY

was awarded the

SENIOR GRADE ONE CERTIFICATE

at GOOD PASS level

OF THE BOARD'S EXAMINATIONS IN SPOKEN ENGLISH

Christabel Burniston

DIRECTOR OF EXAMINATIONS.

DATE 21st July, 1971

Certificates I received for spoken English

Certificate for progress I received at Lavender Hill

Admittedly, some students did attend school pregnant or had to leave school early, but look at it this way: our school, which was labelled a school for unmarried mothers, produced teachers, pharmacists, journalists, musicians, models, preachers, UN members, politicians, nurses, doctors, etc. The list goes on.

These were a couple of the names given to Lavender Hill: 'School for Unmarried Mothers' and 'Mother and Baby Home'.

How can any good come out of Lavender Hill? We proved them wrong.

They have now turned Lavender Hill Secondary School into luxury apartments, housing famous people, but we were there first.

We were like the forgotten few, true Nazarenes. Like Joseph, who was sold into captivity. We were the small axe for the big trees. We were Davids among Goliaths. With the Creator, everything became possible for us.

The first ever Saturday job I had was for just one Saturday in a clothes shop on Clapham Common High Street. My school friend S. Chung was leaving, so she asked if I could replace her. This was all new to me, so I was not needed the next Saturday, but we always looked out for each other.

I then worked in Woolworths, Clapham Junction, after school, on Saturdays and during the school holidays. My parents had then moved to Shakespeare Road, Herne Hill, SE27, as they'd sold their house on Shelgate Road with the intention of moving back to the Caribbean (Jamaica).

After leaving Woolworths I went on to work at Battersea Park Funfair on the candy floss and toffy apple kiosk and also at the gate. PW, HM, RC, and FT were among the crew. Working at the fair allowed you free rides on everything, plus discounts for close friends and family. Night-time was fun after the funfair, as we would stop at the fish and chip shop before going to our yards. There were hardly any troubles. Things were so different to now.

Battersea Park Funfair

I was glad to be out of my parents' house, doing odd jobs to take care of myself, as they treated me so badly. I yearned for Jamaica. My two older brothers were also on their own. They must have spent at least three years in our parents' house before being introduced to factory works.

Most of us Windrush children, especially the males, were sent to a school called Shillington School in Battersea, near Wye Street. Even though they were talented children, our parents and the system did not give them a chance. Boy, did we experience discrimination! We were held back in schools, while some of our parents would threaten us with deportation. What the government did to them, they directed back at us. My parents would say to us that being Jamaican-born, we did not have the same privileges as our English-born siblings. I was constantly told that they should have left us in Jamaica to hardships—hardships I would have welcomed more than the ones we faced in England. Strangely enough, when some went back to the Caribbean they actually went to claim generations-occupied land, throwing the natives off and securing it for God only knows. Some received documents to sign over properties from a well-known attorney in Brown's Town.

After a year or so of living in Herne Hill our parents changed their minds and bought a house back in Battersea on Leathwaite Road. I left school in 1971 with seven CSEs. I got a job working in Boots the Chemist on King's Road, Chelsea, as an assistant on the pharmacist counter. During that time my two brothers were given temporary accommodation back on Leathwaite Road.

I left Leathwaite Road due to bad treatment and went to live in shared accommodation with my secondary school friend ML. Our friend GR's parents gave us a room to share, we had proper cooked foods and we dressed up in the latest fashions, which we brought in Station Approach Candy Fashion, also on King's Road, Chelsea. That was my first taste of freedom.

Battersea Town Hall and the Swan Club above the pub in Stockwell were where we all would meet up. This was funny, as some of our parents would come into the clubs or dances, asking for the lights to be switched on as they were looking for their children or foster children. I remember CC's mother turning up from across the road looking for her, but she hid behind the speakers. There were so many places we could go: places like the Ruby Cinema (where I watched *Enter the Dragon*, starring Bruce Lee, *Shaft*, starring Richard Roundtree and *The Caribbean Fox*) and many youth clubs, such as Providence House, St Mark's Church Hall, Battersea Rise.

CHAPTER FOUR
GOULDEN HOUSE

Goulden House in Battersea was my first flat I could call home. I moved into my newly built flat in 1974 with my son. This was one of the most beautiful homes you could ever imagine. It was a one-bedroom flat with a very large living room, an open-plan kitchen and a bathroom and toilet in one. There was a very long balcony, from where I could watch my son as he grew older playing along with some of my neighbours' children and other children who either lived in Goulden House or had family living there, like a sister from down the way whose sister and mother lived in Goulden House. My son would call her mother 'Grandma'. The play areas were full of activities and were fenced off between younger and older children.

There were times I shared my accommodation with others, as I understood what it was like living at home and the experiences others may have been going through. But some people's intention was to use my address to get on the council list for accommodation. During those times I would actually leave some families, or 'frenemies', in my flat and stay with some good friends. A few of us were very supportive in that way. I have learnt in my life that some people, when they think you are on your own, can take liberties. You get to prove that there's a Creator who watches over you in those times of trial. There were the odd ones whose first reaction when you bumped into them would be, 'You still alive?' One of my sistren would respond, 'Sorry to disappoint you."

Goulden House was what I would now describe as a drop-in centre. There were some who deliberately took it for granted that you were on your own so they took liberties, something I would not dream of doing to them. Families and friends came from all over when I would have them round. This was quite the opposite when they got somewhere of their own, or for those who were already living in their accommodations. There were the 'unwanted visitors' who would just turn up at any time. They would knock the door shouting 'Open the door; it's so and so'. Some would turn up with bad-minded intentions, especially if they thought they could intimidate you in your home with remarks like 'This is council property'. This reminds me of a Trench Town home but in a one-bedroom London flat. Some would see your fruit bowl with one apple and just take it and *nyam* it. Some placed photos on your mantlepiece and when asked whose picture it was would reply that it was their sister who is buried in Putney.

There were meter breakings. Some would rob our children of their Gerber baby food (think about the rents to pay; some had no shame). There was always cooking, eating and music in Goulden House which consisted of other flats, such as original DJ Ital Queens, Coxone, and many more community neighbours. From Goulden House I would look over to Compton House, Surrey Lane, at another friend's flat. When she visited and had to go back to her flat, especially when it was late at night, she would always signal with her light to say she'd reached home safely, as she lived on the eighteenth floor. I also did the same when I visited her flat. I remember these were some of the friends I could go to at any time. They would later become the first girls sound (DJs), built for us by Sir Coxone, who at the time also lived in Goulden House. We had the latest dub plates issued to us by Coxone. Joseph was the queen of writing lyrics in these modern-day times. I would say she has the qualities of a writer. Sister 'S' was the best DJ, highly spiritual, chucky the controller. I was also good with lyrics, with a reserved side to me. Coxone was always inviting over musicians, such as Fredlocks, Dennis Brown, Eeka Mouse, Gregory Issac, and many more. We would play Lousia Marks's songs. She was one of the Queens of Lover's Rock. Lousia Marks had some great songs. One of her 'number one tunes', as they were called at the time, was 'Caught You in a Lie'. This was what you called a tune;

it would be played on all sound systems, especially Sir Coxone, Highway Hi-Fi, Sufferah Sound, Danny King, Lord David, I Spy, and Mighty Redeemer from Rowan Crescent.

There were times when someone did not want to be recognised in a club, so we would change their Afro into cornrow plaits.

Across the river we would visit St Mark's Hall in Ladbrooke Grove, West London. On Latimer Road were the West London clubs. In White City and Shepherd's Bush were clubs that would be visited by the Wailers. Moving back over to South London was the Twelve Tribes' headquarters at St Agnes Place, between Kennington and Brixton. These were some of the well-known clubs: Four Aces, Bouncing Ball and Mr B's. There were the usual *shub-ins* run by a lady called Aunty Janet based at the Junction. There you would buy a plate of curried goat and rice for one pound. Drinks, a pound. Plus, you would be expected to pay at the door. Oh yes, we've always had our bouncers start off in houses. I knew Lousia and her sister. We came a long way. Her sister and I were in the mother and baby home in Sutton, Surrey, where she gave birth to her daughter and I to my son.

RIP, Louisa. Lovers rock lives on. (See short poems, which relate to the above and below.)

I remember Chapmans Agency on Webb's Road where we would queue up for catering jobs. We were sent all over the place, especially to banks and insurance companies and other well-named companies. In a few of the places we would serve teas from these massive pots they called tea urns, pushing them into lifts to take to the offices.

These were some of the things we did to help out with our children. One of the Ital Queens pulled me up one day and said, 'Sis, I know you're a dresser. Make sure you dress your son in the latest fashion. Up to this day my son is a fashion statement. Joseph (EC) are to be blamed, as my son now thinks he's on the catwalk. Princess Head also carried the swing in the 1970s, with a much smaller market, where you would get lots of fruits and veggies. There was George's shop, which sold Afro-Caribbean food. Wilfred from the Caribbean worked there and eventually took over the shop when George died.

Most shops were in competition, issuing food-stamp books that could be exchanged for food once they were filled. It was similar to the present-day Tesco Clubcard, Sainsbury's Nectar points, and others.

During those times, Northcote Road would top all the supermarket names, such as Selco, Tesco, etc. The butcher's shop at the bottom of Cains Road sold mutton, oxtails, cows' foot and this boiler chicken that was set apart for our Sunday dinners.

Cains Road, Battersea

The pub on Northcote was where you would find the older generation congregating. This pub should have been named the Afro-Caribbean pub. That's where they would run a community savings scheme called Partners, a savings scheme that did not involve going to the bank. Nowadays there are all different names for this kind of savings, including pyramids and get-rich-quick schemes. There were at least twenty people who would join, and each would get a weekly hand or draw.

Throwing or joining a Partner would sometimes create problems, escalating in fights, as there was sometimes mistrust. You would hear stories of people running off with people's draws, enabling them to purchase land abroad or build houses.

Uncle Bull, Uncle Brown, Uncle Poppy, the Davises and many more were regulars at the Northcote Pub. Other pubs included the famous Plough on St John's Hill Road. We had Foster and Pendley, with their Afro-Caribbean shop on Battersea Rise. Our community had a bakery shop on the corner of Mallison Road, facing Lena Supermarket, an ice-cream shop next to the One-Arm Bandit, a gambling arcade, then the famous fish shop where we would buy our snappers, salt fish and bream. There was no shortage of food stalls selling yams, plantains, sweet potatoes—all fresh food shipped over from Africa and the Caribbean. All along Northcote Road were every kind of stall—very cosmopolitan. We cannot forget the famous Harding and Hobbs, the cousin store to Peter Jones. Harding and Hobbs (renamed Debenhams) had a Bargain Basement where you were able to equip your home with affordable utensils and house products. Today's Poundland is no match for Bargain Basement.

Mallinson Road, Battersea

Northcote Road is now an area called 'Second Chelsea', with all the continental bars and yuppies, who moved in after most of the Windrush generation retired back to the Caribbean, pushed out of the market and transferred to Croydon and the outskirts of London. It is very sad to know and experience that due to discrimination in society some of us lost jobs, homes, and status because of our nationality and status.

Inside a typical home of the Windrush generation in the 1960s and 1970s

In March 1977 I gave birth to my second child at the Princess Beatrice Hospital in Kensington. That year I was given a three-bedroom, new home in Wandsworth. I was still putting up family and friends in my new home. There were incidents where some would use our address for dental care bills, which would now carry a fine for fraud. They would turn up with missing teeth, then the next time they came they had gold teeth in their mouths. Some who had bad credit used your details. If they were stopped for any kind of wrong, they would give others' names and addresses. Some took kindness for weakness. I believe this is down to a lot of experiences living in bed and breakfasts and Nightingale Square for the homeless.

Believe it or not, I always held down jobs, although some people think they helped support me and my children. I think some people thought I wouldn't survive.

In 1979 I gave birth to my last child, another daughter, at St Thomas's Hospital, Lambeth.

In 1980 I worked at the DHSS in Wandsworth. Before moving to Wandsworth, my son started school in Latchmere Infant School, Battersea. He made everyone laugh on his first day. After school I asked him the name of his teacher. He responded by saying that her name is Miss Kakafart (Karachi).

In Wandsworth the girls went to Waverton Nursery, which is now a development of new houses and flats, then on to Swaffield School with their brother and cousin, my nephew. His mother was from the Hackney area of East London, but he spent time between me and my younger sister before going to live with his grandmother in Hackney, East London, He was always in touch with the other side of his family in South London; he spent most of his childhood there.

After working at the DHSS I went on to further education in East Croydon to learn office skills, then I was with a company for seventeen years. Following that I took a career break, during which I attended South Thames College and studied fashion and textiles. I then worked in the Civil Service for over twenty-two years until I retired. And now I have decided to write about my life experience and my move from Stepney to London.

My nephews are always sending messages or words for thoughts:

Try getting it on your own rather than someone reminding you of what they did for you.

Your mind is like a magnet—when you think of blessings you will attract blessings—so don't go there with problems.

And yet I (we) rise. Our Creator is real.

The mouth speaks the things that are in the heart.

Good people have good things in their hearts, so they say good things. Evil people have evil in their hearts, so they say evil things.

Pray to the Creator for knowledge (to know),

Wisdom to be wise and understanding (overstand).

Words are powerful tools that can build or tear down.

Boastful words are insecure to the heart.

The right words spoken at the right time and in the right way can bring order in the midst of confusion.

Notice how some people look shocked when they see you. They can't believe it's you. Curses cannot harm (hurt) you 'cause you don't deserve it. They're like birds, perched on trees, fences and roofs but cannot settled: they will get up and fly away.

Good people know the right things to say.

If you want to know what others think about you, watch the signs and actions on their children's countenance.

Check ourselves before we speak. Humbleness is power.

(Some quotes taken from the Book of Proverbs)

CONTROL YOUR TONGUE!

1. WHEN SOMEONE GOSSIP, MARK THAT PERSON.
2. THEY WILL TALK TO YOU ABOUT SOMEBODY ELSE.
3. THEY WILL TALK TO SOMEBODY ELSE ABOUT YOU.
4. WHEN SOMEONE IS HASTY IN THEIR WORDS, THERE IS MORE HOPE FOR A FOOL.
5. TAKE TIME TO GET FACTS, THEN MOST OF THE TIME YOU WILL SPEAK DIFFERENTLY.
6. E.G. HANNAH PRAY FOR A CHILD AND ELI THE HIGH PRIEST THOUGHT SHE WAS DRUNK.
7. THE DISCIPLES SAW JESUS WALKING ON WATER THEY NEVER KNEW WHAT TO THINK.
8. PRAY BEFORE YOU JUMP TO CONCLUSIONS
9. A FLATTERING TONGUE THERE IS NO FAITHFULLNESS IN THEIR MOUTH; THEY ONLY FLATTER WITH THEIR TONGUE.
10. SAY WHAT YOU MEAN AND MEAN WHAT YOU SAY, BE GENUINE.
11. WHEN YOU FLATTER PEOPLE YOU MANIPULATE THEM FOR YOUR OWN ENDS. DON'T DO THAT, TELL THEM STRAIGHT, AND IF YOU LOVE THEM BE TRUTHFUL WITH THEM.
12. A JUDGEMENTAL TONGUE: JESUS SAID JUDGE NOT THAT YOU BE NOT JUDGED.
13. FOR WITH WHAT JUDGEMENT YOU JUDGE, YOU WILL BE JUDGE WITH THE MEASURE YOU USE.
14. IT WILL MEASURE BACK TO YOU.
15. DO NOT BE QUICK TO CONDEMN OTHERS. THE TRUTH IS, HOW YOU DEAL WITH OTHER PEOPLE DETERMINES HOW GOD DEALS WITH YOU.

IF YOU KNOW YOU'RE ON THE RIGHT TRACK OR TRYING TO BE RIGHT, AND THEN SAY THANK YOU JESUS.

AMEN.

Baby Mothers for Convenience

Times were hard, as rough as could be. Mothers and children tried their best to survive. Benefits were a help, but it depended on how you used them.

Think about the rent to pay. Some of us lived nowhere. Survival was the game.

I can still remember very clearly the five of us. We would try our hands at most things, from Chapman's Agency to an all-girls sound (Queens of the West, aka Ital Queens). Some were for us, some against us. Still, it was a challenge.

We took pride in our children and ourselves.

They tried to use us baby mothers for convenience. They came searching for food which they could not provide. Some tried to control our homes, but we would not let them.

Our children, they thought, would be an investment, even though they had no thoughts of contributions, hoping that when their children came of age, they would provide for them.

Our children learnt from us the meaning of pride and dignity. Even though some may have fallen along the way, their roots are still firm.

Wake up, wake up, to a conscious mind. Start to respect before you run out of time and mind.

CHAPTER FIVE
ME, MYSELF AND I

Throughout my whole life I have gone to church. Stepney Baptist Church was the first and main church I ever attended. We had the main service at 10 am until after 12 pm. Then we went back for the evening service. This would depend on certain events. Harvest time was a big celebration, when the church would be decorated with canes, banana leaves, coconut leaves and plants of all kinds. People would bring in foods from their grounds (fields) and they would sing bringing in the sheaves: 'We shall come rejoicing bringing in the sheaves.' I don't really know what happened to those foods? The singing was out of this world. The Downies would raise the roof with singing and the playing of instruments. Baptism was fun to see, how some people would dress up in white and the preacher dipped them into the pool. That was on a Sunday. The next day some of those said people did some cussings; you would never have thought they'd have been baptised the day before. Two of the songs that still stick in my head are 'Just As I am' and 'Take My Life and Let It Be'. Teacher James was one of the overseers for the church, as well as the headmaster for Stepney School.

The other main church was down at the bottom, behind Miss Naomi's shop and opposite Mr Tai and Miss Norah's shop. This church was a Pentecostal church, where my other grandmother Ann Brown attended. To tell the truth, we never saw much of her, but when we went to that service sometimes in the evening, we would glimpse her. That church was on fire, with the beating of drums, knocking of tambourines, wheel and turn—spiritually, you could almost relate it to a Pocomania way of worshipping. After years of being in England and visiting some churches of African descent, I then related to Stepney Tabernacle Church. I have also noticed spiritual ways with lots of the Jamaican/Caribbean artists.

I have been on a physical and spiritual journey, where I've read the words and, at that time, not understood certain meanings. For instance, there's a verse written by David the Psalmist when he was going through some trials. He said, 'When thy mother and father forsake thee, then the Lord will take thee up.' I now see this verse to mean substitute helpers/careers. I can relate to a Nigerian family living on Stormont Road as a substitute family in my life. Ghanaians were also a strong spiritual support in my life. They were angels in human form, coming together with physical and spiritual searchings. There are places of worships where you have to be on the alert, in case of being led. Try the spirit and pray earnestly to seek and communicate with the Creator, as many are called but few are chosen. Experience is a very expensive school on a spiritual journey.

(See my son's spiritual paintings on p. 57 of a Lamb and scroll.)

Myself and the Bishop

CHAPTER SIX
COMING TO AMERICA

On Thursday, 5 May 1994, we arrived at John F. Kennedy International Airport, New York. We took a connecting flight to Philadelphia International Airport. We were picked up by a friend (a Stepney connection who now lives in the USA). We were driven to his apartment in Wilmington, Delaware. Once we had unpacked, we went to meet up with some Guyanese friends and have some Caribbean food. We then rang our family in London to say we'd arrived safely. I rang some friends in New York who used to live in Battersea and had emigrated to the USA.

On Friday, 6 May, we met Gloria, Mrs Brown and some families who'd know our family in Stepney and Calderwood. Later on during the day, Gloria took us to the shopping mall Sears.

On Saturday, 7 May, we went shopping on our own. During the evening we went to another shopping mall to watch a movie but then changed our minds and went for a meal instead. It rained that night. I never knew the Americans could eat so much. I thought the platter of food was for all four of us, only to be told it was for one person. We took the rest back to the apartment.

On Sunday, 8 May, we went to church. During the night, some of us went to a reggae club. On the Monday we took the Greyhound bus into Rodney Square, a very beautiful place, then we returned to Calder Boulevard. On the same day, in the afternoon, we went into Philly. We brought back burgers and chips to eat in the apartment.

Before we left London for Philly, a friend, Elaine, had sent over some of her designer t-shirts for the families. They asked about her and my family back in London.

Some mornings, we would be taken out for breakfast, which was different. When we did not go out for meals, we would sometimes cook ackee and salt fish, which they loved. After our meals we would go to the store to buy drinks. During the days, we were so used to going out on our own, as the Americans hold down two jobs, so the weekend was their time to take us around. But we found our way quite easily. It's like living in London. We loved going shopping and buying things for family and friends back in London.

During some of our trips in the parks we came across entertainment and we would eat burgers and fries. We met up with a project leader and had chats regarding the youth of Delaware. He had on display some of the things they'd made in their workshops. I also promised to visit him before returning to London. On our way back to get the Greyhound we stopped in a Caribbean restaurant to sample their sweet potato pie. Buju tapes were selling like hot cakes, so we brought some back for my son.

During the evening, there were sometimes visitors while some of us were in another room. Gloria, and sometimes Pablo, would take us to Sears, as they never worked. Pablo was a backing guitarist playing for different gigs. We met up with Gloria's uncle from miles away; now he lives on the other side of Delaware, a place call Newcastle. We also met Suzie, who was originally from Calderwood, St Ann. The following evening we all went for a meal at an air base.

During the second week of our stay we went into New Jersey, to a place called Atlantic City. It was a massive place by the sea with a pier and all sorts of entertainment. On our way back into Delaware, we stopped off at a family gathering, where we met up with one of Buster Brown's sons, Paul.

Our family in the States were really nice to us. We promised to meet up but never got round to seeing them. Desmond, who used to live in Nottingham, England and now lives in Atlanta, wanted to meet up with us in Florida, but there was not enough time.

On 16 May we experienced a confrontation in Delaware Court, with some pastor suing another pastor for $5,000. I got to learn that they sue you for anything in the USA.

On 19 May we said our farewells, took a flight to Washington and then on to London.

It was such a blessing to arrive back home to my children, family and friends. Give the Almighty thanks.

Since that trip, I have had some of our American friends visit us here in London, and also a reunion in Jamaica.

CHAPTER SEVEN
BACK HOME

In 1983 I sent my son to relatives in Jamaica during the school holidays, one of whom was Leah (aka Aneita Downie), who raised me, my brothers and my cousins until we emigrated. My brother and his son were already there, spending up to six months, but my son was spending just six weeks. My son went on the same flight as some family friends, the Browns, who were going to Clarendon. S made sure she visited my son in Calderwood, as they were coming back on the same flight to London.

My cousin Leah, who helped raise me before my move to England. May she RIP.

My son had a memorable time in Jamaica. He became more advanced with his drawings and paintings and Leah took him all over, showing him places I used to run up and down. I rang him once a week to see how he was getting on. He was certainly missed by his sisters, who would eventually visit Jamaica over next couple of years.

Photo of the home I was born in in Jamaica

When my son arrived back in England his suitcase was full of yams, banana, cocoa and sweet potatoes. When asked what happened to his clothes, he said that certain relatives who used to live abroad handed his clothes to family members saying that when he got back to England I could replace them. This did not surprise me, as they never wanted to see us—those who left Jamaica—progress. Yes, I was vexed, considering how hard I'd worked to accommodate all my children, being a one-parent family, but never mind, God is able. I did not mind if his clothes went to Leah's children in Stepney, as she had raised me till the age of eleven.

In 1985 I took my first trip back to Jamaica in twenty years. I was excited to be going back to my place of birth with my two daughters. My uncle, along with Jakey, Miss Neita's (a Stepney School teacher) son came and picked us up from Montego Bay Sangster International Airport. The flight was good. My daughter Allison kept on coming up to me and saying 'He's not dead'. I was wondering what she was talking about until, when the plane landed, I recognised Jimmy Cliff from 'The Harder They Come', and this was who Allison was talking about. He was on the same flight. We insisted on having his autograph. His commented, 'Twenty years since you left Jamaica', then he looked at my daughter and said she reminded him of his British-born daughter whose name also began with 'A'. He said he knew Stepney, Calderwood, Miles and Alva quite well.

Journeying along the north coast was a picture. At that time, we did not have dual carriageways or motorways. We drove within the parishes and districts. We could see the different parishes, with street dances, open-air revellers, people selling food on the roadsides, drinking, and dominoes being played outside shops. Yes, I was home in Jamaica. We drove through Montego Bay, into Falmouth, Duncan, Discovery Bay, my parish (St Ann), through Brown's Town, into the hills and on to Calderwood and Stepney.

Some of the returnees were not pleased to see me in Jamaica 'cause they knew I would tell about the bad treatment they had put us through in England. The family I had left behind was so glad to see me return home. You should have seen how some of the returnees handed out gifts like they had provided them. Now all of a sudden there were relatives appearing out of nowhere telling me how they used to help mind me. Okay, but I only remembered Leah, Aunt Lou, Muma and Papa.

It was so strange to see some faces coming up to me looking overjoyed and saying, '*Laud God, luk pon little Lena. She nu grow.*' That was coming from Aunt Zen, as she was known in the district. Her home was neighbouring Taylor Bye's shop, a well-to-do family in the district. Before I left the district I used to hear the names John and Prixie, her two sons who lived in London. In my later years in London I was blessed to meet them and they remembered me and my brothers very well.

It was good to see some of my school friends still in the district, like Punchae, Geeson, the McDonalds, Miss Jen from Calderwood, Cousin Dittah (the Bygraves). Cousin Uton came all the way from Ochi Rios to get me and the girls and take us back to his home. Three of his children and his wife, Pauline, were with him. His children and my daughters ran all over Shaw Park Gardens climbing nutmeg and almond trees until they were told to come down by a security guard. We went into the bank in Ochi, changed some money and opened an account with VMB. My cousin came up to me in the bank and generously said that I could always put his name on my account, so that he could manage it while I was in Foreign. I now see why they call English people mad.

I glimpsed my Cousin Olive's brother, Beeda (may they now RIP). I was with Leah a lot of the time, as her son Ricky was staying over in Calderwood along with one of Miss Cook's grandsons (Shortie). Leah was constantly back and forth, washing, cleaning and cooking for both returnees' family members. I did all my washing myself while in Jamaica.

The reason I stayed over at my other grandparents' house was because I was not aware that the home in Berry Hill was in ruins. It was a shame that the returnees could not help to restore the houses. It was emotional for me to stand over my grandparents, with my cousins Uton and Leah bringing back memories. The same thing happened when I walked to the Lawrence home to be told that my best friend in class had passed. She was so bright. There were two other students, Janet Nelson and Agnes Parks, who

I was told lived in a different parish. I heard that Lena McDonald emigrated to the USA. Elizabeth's brother Larry was also around for me to see. I use to play jacks outside their shop pavement.

My children loved travelling on the minibuses to hear 'One stop, driver' or have ten people in a four-door vehicle. That was exciting for them. They loved the box meals; they loved all the meals in Jamaica. I was introduced to my cousin Buster Brown, who also ran the club in Nine Miles, in one of his stores in Brown's Town. I took my daughters in to Stepney School, which I'd once attended, and to my surprise, there was Miss Neita still teaching. I was asked to leave the girls with her in her class, but only Dionie wanted to stay. Imagine how I felt to be back in Jamaica and see my daughters in school.

> Stepney All Age School,
> Calderwood P.O.
> St. Ann.
> Jamaica W.I.
> 2nd. March, 1987.
>
> My dear Miss Newby,
>
> Greetings and best wishes for the season.
>
> I received your letter with cash enclosed. Thanks so much on behalf of the pupils, staff and myself.
>
> We are now near to Two Thousand dollars. We were thinking of starting a lunch room but we were advised not to start any building as they will be remodelling the whole building. They should have started from May of last year. We are still optimistic they will do some work this year and we could use cash to buy a refrigerator for the school.
>
> You are doing a wonderful job for your country. Kindly convey additional thanks to all those who contributed.
>
> May the Good Lord continue to richly bless you.
>
> Your past teacher,
> L. Nette.

We went to the Baptist church on a Sunday. I noticed the girls would not keep still, and when asked what was the matter, they both pointed to a lizard on one of the seats. You want to see the type of worshippers in these churches, but as the saying goes, 'Nuff *a wi* are called but only the chosen few, Amen.'

We would sometimes walk through the bushes to visit Uncle Brown down at the bottom of Nine Miles and sit on his verandah talking with Smithie and listening to music blaring out of Busta Club, where people danced to 'Girlie, Girlie' by Sophie George, while doing the Scabbie.

My sibling came down from Kingston with her sister to stay in Grandfather Newby's house; apparently this was what she did regularly. My brother Smart, who later passed, was also around. They called him the 'bad boy in the district', as he had a reputation. My grandfather's brother, Uncle Joe's, wife (aka as Miss Tit) was still going strong. So was Miss Una. When it came to favouritism, Rodney was Uncle Joe's favourite, Philip and June were Mass Johnnie's, while I was spoilt by the Downies.

Uncle and Aunty would always come to the gate to take me and the girls for rides. We would stop in restaurants in Brown's Town, *nam* plenty of food, eat our bellies full then back to Calderwood and Stepney. On a Sunday we would picnic at Dunn's River Falls. Nuff admirations was so visible for foreign travels (please, I was born, yah), even though they still look at you as foreigners. What can you say? They called you a foreigner in England, and now Jamaica!

Uncle Bull had a beautiful house in Alexandria (aka Charlton). He was living with some young girl call Yvonne. A few years after, it was reported that her brothers took his life. So sad. It was also rumoured that he built a little house for her. It's not just in Jamaica these things happen, so you have to be wise in your walks of life, as karma is real.

A couple of days before leaving, Uncle and Aunt killed a goat. We had Manish water soup and mutton and rice, which was nice of them. I cried yet again leaving Jamaica. I supposed it was flashbacks from my childhood memories.

In 1987 family members visited England ex-repats. I then went back to Jamaica in 1988, after Hurricane Gilbert, which took place in the September, this time with my nephew, my son and my daughters. We flew to Miami and took a connecting flight with Air Jamaica. We had problems through customs as we landed in Montego bay. We had two suitcases each. Everyone had their suitcases except my nephew. After waiting around, the workers told us that some of the luggage was still in Miami but they would be delivered the next day to Calderwood. They certainly did deliver my nephew's suitcases—with three quarters of the food missing!

Foreigner: 1988 flight from London Heathrow. We arrived at Montego Bay Airport at 7 pm Jamaica time. Coming through customs I noticed that all my relatives were outside to meet us. The van that had come to pick us up was completely full, with even some unwanted guests. Some people just do not have any shame. There was hardly enough space for us to sit. Some of us had to use the suitcases as seats. The driver of the van went by the name of Daugh (dog). He told everyone to make themselves small, for us to find seats. We journeyed along the north coast watching the sunset and smelling the freshly cooked food on the roadside. As we journeyed into St Ann all you could hear was music coming from shops, houses and street dancing. As the bright yellow van cruised along the north coast I noticed how everyone we were with had not a care in the world. One of my daughters and my nephew were sitting on some of the suitcases, which was quite fun for them. We had travelled with ten suitcases altogether. That was just after Hurricane Gilbert. Come to think of it, it was not as bad as when you saw it on TV. Everyone seemed to have coped quite well. As I sat looking around in the van, I was very pleased to see most of my relatives. But looking at their faces, they were more pleased to see the ten suitcases.

As we began to approach Brown's Town, I had to ask everyone if they were going to contribute towards the fare, which I believe was 375 JMD—that was what Daugh, the driver, had asked for. I made it quite clear that they would not be having excursions at my expense. You could see the looks on their faces. Some of them couldn't wait to see those suitcases opened. Before approaching

Calderwood Post Office, some shouted out, 'One stop, driver.' Daugh let them off one by one. When we got to my grandfather's house, some of the families were there, like Mr Star, Blacktoe and Raymond. We got there at around 9 pm Jamaica time.

The next day a relative who was on holiday from London came round to see us. Her mother only lived around the corner. Returnees from England. My children and nephew had such good times. Living in the house was a teacher who taught at Murray Mount All Age School. The children would go with him to school for the experience. To them it was different, but good fun, as they made lots of friends. This reminded me of a couple years back when my youngest daughter attended Stepney School, but this time it was Murray School.

There was never a dull moment for the children. They were very adventurous and were all over the places—Nine Miles, Stepney, Calderwood, Stirling, Alva, and some of their favourite spots, such as Grand Mountain. During the day, me and my cousins would be taxi driven almost everywhere— beaches, Purto cico, Green Grotto. We hung out a lot in Brown's Town, Claremont and Cave Valley. It was funny having to push onto these buses (not so any more). It was a picture. No one was left behind. We made room for everyone. I spent about six weeks in Jamaica on that visit.

As you travel throughout the island, you are greeted as foreigners—the same as in England. I had to tell these people that 'I may live in Foreign but I am from Jamaica, born and raised in Berry Hill, Stepney, St Ann'.

One of the strangest things was that people had changed. Some moved out to other parishes and districts, and to foreign countries. Some of the ones who were still there (not all) expected a lot from you. The reason was that a lot of us who lived abroad had been giving them the wrong information about our lives. We'd lie and brag that we owned trains and that we lived a stone's throw from Buckingham Palace. We'd take pictures standing next to some well-to-do people with their fancy houses and cars and lie, saying they were ours. So when I told them how long it had taken me to save to get back home, they thought I was just saying it and they turned around and called me a 'mad English woman'. By the time I had finished with some of them, *they* were treating *me* instead, as they felt sorry for me. I must admit pulling some scam, being driven almost everywhere and promising to file for them when I got back to Foreign. They would also do the same thing, hiding their partners or sometimes saying they were their relatives, to get to Foreign. There were some genuine ones—they weren't all scammers—but as the sayings go, 'one bad apple spoils the whole bunch' and 'we should not judge a book by its cover'. I heard some of the women bragging that once their partners landed in Foreign they would follow shortly. I sometimes had to point out that milk and honey is not where I was coming from. There was stress, low-paid jobs, bad housing conditions, detention centres—certainly not Butlin's. There were convenient institutions, brutalities. The fortunate ones in Jamaica should dream about how to invest academically, spiritually. Our future lies in our hands. We need strong foundations, respect, economy, with spiritual and natural growth. That's one of the visions I see for Jamaica. Not just for Jamaica, but for all the Caribbean islands.

Before leaving the island my son was riding a relative's bike and fell off in some gully, cutting the side of his face. He had to be taken to Charlton Hospital, where he was given an injection, which was costly due to the fact I had not taken out insurance. That was a lesson I learnt.

We left the island early, via Miami and then on to London. The relative whose bike he'd had the accident on came to see us before we left, reminding us that his bicycle needed to be fixed. You see some people's faces; you don't see their minds. His bike was more important than my son's accident.

After so many visits to Jamaica I realised that all-inclusive was much more comfortable and relaxing. To me, that is a proper holiday. You then see how the other half lives. And that's exactly how it is when I visit other countries. No one is telling you they don't know what they're going to cook or inviting you for a meal and telling you they don't have meat kind. I hold reasonable conversations in these complexes. I still visit but I don't stop overnight.

This is entirely down to each individual supporting the locals. The wages may not be that great, but at least it gives the locals employment so they can help themselves within the economy.

Many times while staying in all-inclusives, I come across holidaymakers from the USA and Canada. When we start talking, I realise that some of us have the same district connections. In the Grand Bahia I met workers in the gifts shops who told me that their father, Daugh, from Murray had actually picked me up from Montego Bay when I'd stayed with relatives. One of the reps was my family member. There was a receptionist, and stall holders who would come into the grounds to sell their craft. You may not be putting a great deal into the economy but every little helps.

CHAPTER EIGHT

MY CHILDREN AND GRANDCHILDREN

Cheri Blair presenting me with a certificate

Me on the cover of the Jamaican edition of *Vogue*

As a baby my son went to nursery in Winders Road, Battersea, then Oldrige Road, Balham, then he was back in Battersea with daily minders. He went to Latchmere Infant School and Swaffield Primary School.

After leaving primary school, my son went to Ernest Bevin Secondary School. Academically, he was an outstanding student in graphics and design. He was extremely good at designing trainers. He did work experience at some art classes, which took him all the way to North London. His work in art saw him drawing and designing bookmarks and spiritual paintings, entering drawing competitions and designing logos for some well-known companies, including the one I worked for for seventeen years. He got into De Montfort University in Leicester, where he developed his talents. When he came back to London he worked at Cordwainers, City of London. He's now a qualified design and technology teacher.

Samples of my son's drawings

My first daughter came to Wandsworth from Battersea at a young age (seven months), where she went to Waverton Day Nursery then on to Swaffield Infant and Primary School. She later went to Fulham Cross Secondary School, South Thames College then on to WBC where she is now a project manager.

My second daughter started nursery at about four months old, when she joined her sister at Waverton Day Nursery. She, like the others, went to Swaffield Infant and Primary School. ADT was her secondary school (which is now known as Ashcroft Academy). She went to Richmond College then Roehampton University, where she gained experience in marketing and business. Pride Magazines and GQ were two of the places she worked. She has been to New Orleans annual festive activities, as well those held as in London. She took me to meet with Iyanla Vanzant (well famous with 'Yesterday I Cried'). I have learnt so much listening to this wonderful spiritual soul.

Even though there have been challenging times with my children, I pray to the Almighty that better must come.

Two of my grandchildren have been through university, while the others are still in primary.

I have noticed that some will always like to put you down, especially when they see how well you have coped. They want to take your credit. For example, some say they were in better position than I was, so they helped me out.

There will always be others around who use your home as a drop-in centre if you let them.

The only time I did not work was during maternity leave. My children were well known for attending play centres during school breaks. As they got older they used to help out with family and friends' children, especially my older daughter. I could then see the qualities coming from their great-grandparents.

Quote from one of my nephew's updates: 'Accept the people as they are, but place them where they belong.'

Keep That Someone

Who will always help you through in times of trouble and despair?

Whose thoughts are sometimes shared with you when you're down and out?

Whose help will never cost a dime and always be there with a listening ear?

With never a thought of betrayal in mind, who could ask for more?

Some will come when you are down to help you see your troubles through,

To see how down you really are and wonder if it's really you.

But on their way, they will laugh and say, 'You see, I told you so,

'I knew he had it coming soon. You see, I told you so.'

Some will say how good you look, while others laugh at you,

Even though they envy you, they wish they could be you.

Some will laugh, some will talk with bitterness in their hearts,

With eyes as poisoned as ivy, they would like to see you down.

Some will get you off the hook, while others nail you to it,

Some will help you through the years, so why not keep that someone with you?

Lightning Source UK Ltd.
Milton Keynes UK
UKHW051104060223
416527UK00011B/410